MY FIRST B

NORWAY

ALL ABOUT NORWAY FOR KIDS

GLOBED
CHILDREN BOOKS

Interior and cover Design: Daniel Day
Editor: Margaret Bam

For My Sons, Daniel, David and Jude

Alesund, Norway

Norway

Norway is a **country**.

A country is land that is controlled by a **single government**. Countries are also called **nations, states, or nation-states**.

Countries can be **different sizes**. Some countries are big and others are small.

Trondheim, Norway

Where Is Norway?

Norway is located in the continent of **Europe.**

A continent is **a massive area of land that is separated from others by water or other natural features**.

Norway is situated in Northern Europe.

Lofoten Islands, Norway

Capital

The capital of Norway is Oslo.

Oslo is located in the **south-eastern part** of the country.

Oslo is the largest city in Norway and is known for its rich history, scenic waterfront, and vibrant cultural scene, with numerous museums, parks, and landmarks to explore.

Trolltunga, Norway

Cities and Regions

Norway can be divided into 11 administrative regions called counties.

The regions of Norway are:

Oslo, Rogaland, Møre og Romsdal, Nordland, Viken, Innlandet, Vestfold og Telemark, Agder, Vestland, Trøndelag and Troms og Finnmark.

Norwegian girl

Population

Norway has population of around **5 million people** making it the 144th most populated country in the world and the 25th most populated country in Europe.

Size

Norway is **385,207 square kilometres** making it the 61st largest country in the world and the sixth largest country in Europe.

Some of the major cities in Norway include Bergen, Stavanger, Trondheim, and Tromsø.

Languages

The national languages of Norway are Norwegian and Sami.

Kven, Romani, Scandoromani and Norwegian sign language are the regional languages of Norway.

Here are a few Norwegian phrases and sayings
- **Vær så god** - You're welcome
- **Vær så snill** - Please
- **Unnskyld meg** - Excuse me

The Vigeland Park, Oslo, Norway

Attractions

There are lots of interesting places to see in Norway.

Some beautiful places to visit in Norway are

- **The Vigeland Park**
- **Viking Ship Museum**
- **Akershus Fortress**
- **The Norwegian Museum of Cultural History**
- **Bryggen**
- **The Royal Palace**

Flam, Norway

History of Norway

Norway has a long and fascinating history with evidence of human presence dating back to the Stone Age. It is believed that humans have inhabited the area from as early as 11,000 to 8,000 BC.

Norway entered into a union with Denmark in 1397, and remained a part of the Danish kingdom for over 400 years. Norway gained independence from Sweden in 1905 and was invaded by Nazi Germany in 1940 and occupied for five years.

Christmas in Oslo

Customs in Norway

Norway has many fascinating customs and traditions.

- Norway has a rich tradition of folk music and dance, with various regional styles and instruments such as the Hardanger fiddle, a traditional Norwegian violin. Folk dances such as the "springar" and "halling" are often performed during celebrations and events.
- Christmas is a significant holiday in Norway. One popular Christmas tradition is "julebord," which is a Christmas party or feast where families and friends gather to enjoy traditional Christmas foods.

Bergen, Norway

Music of Norway

There are many different music genres in Norway such as **Dansband, Nordic folk music, Norwegian hip hop and Joik.**

Some notable Norwegian musicians include
- **AURORA - A Norwegian singer, songwriter and record producer**
- **Astrid S - A Norwegian singer and songwriter who placed fifth in the Norwegian version of Pop Idol**
- **Sigrid - A Norwegian singer-songwriter who released two studio albums called Sucker Punch and How to Let Go**

Food of Norway

Norwegian food is known for being delicious, flavourful and colourful.

The national dish of Norway is **Mutton and Cabbage Stew,** a dish of slow-cured lamb leg.

Lutefisk served with pea puree, potatoes and bacon

Food of Norway

Norwegian cuisine is known for its emphasis on fresh and locally sourced ingredients, particularly fish and seafood due to Norway's extensive coastline.

Some popular dishes in Norway include

- **Lutefisk: Consists of dried fish served with boiled potatoes, peas, bacon, and white sauce.**
- **Rakfisk: A dish of fermented fish**
- **Klippfisk: Dried and salted cod that is rehydrated and cooked with potatoes.**

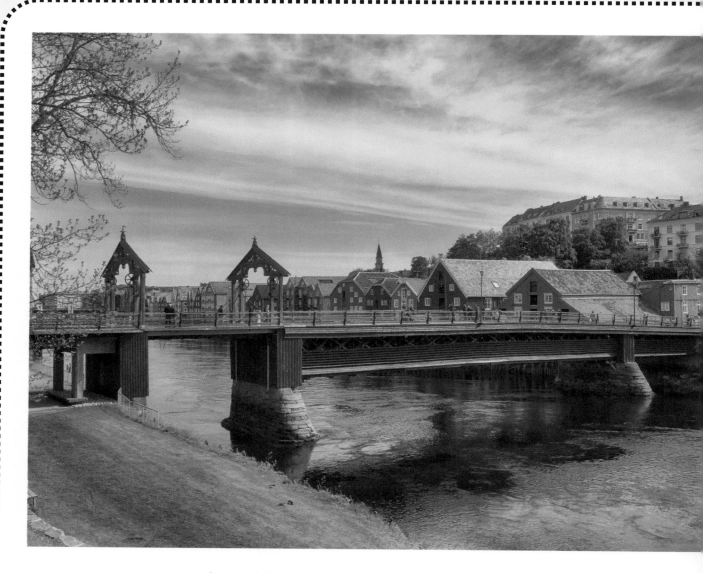

The Old Bridge, Trondheim, Norway

Weather in Norway

Norway experiences a combination of coastal and continental climates, with cooler temperatures and higher precipitation in the west and milder temperatures in the south and southeast.

Northern Norway, including the Arctic regions of Norway, experiences subarctic and tundra climates. Winters are long, cold, and dark, with temperatures often well below freezing, while summers are short with cool temperatures.

The coldest months fall between **December to February.**

Reindeer in Norway

Animals of Norway

There are many wonderful animals in Norway.

Here are some animals that live in Norway

- **Norwegian Forest Cat**
- **Reindeer**
- **Elk**
- **Arctic fox**
- **Polar bear (in Svalbard, an archipelago under Norwegian sovereignty).**

Kjeragbolten, Norway

Mountains

There are many beautiful mountains in Norway which is one of the reasons why so many people visit this beautiful country every year.

Here are some of Norway's mountains

- **Galdhøpiggen**
- **Ulriken**
- **Kjerag**
- **Glittertind**
- **Torghatten**

Football with Norway Flag

Sports of Norway

Sports play an integral part in Norwegian culture. The most popular sport is **Football.**

Here are some of famous sportspeople from Norway

- **Karsten Warholm - Athletics**
- **Jakob Ingebrigtsen - Athletics**
- **Kjetil André Aamodt - Skiing**
- **Marit Bjørgen - Skiing**
- **Thor Hushovd - Racer**
- **Martin Ødegaard - Football**

Edvard Hagerup Grieg

Famous

Many successful people hail from Norway.

Here are some notable Norwegian figures

- **Ole Gunnar Solskjær – Footballer**
- **Edvard Hagerup Grieg – Composer**
- **Henrik Ibsen – Playwright**
- **Fridtjof Nansen – Polymath**
- **Morten Harket – Musician**

Northern Lights, Aurora Borealis, Norway

Something Extra...

As a little something extra, we are going to share some lesser known facts about Norway

- Norway is one of the world's happiest countries.
- Constitution Day which is known as "Syttende Mai" in Norwegian, is the National Day of Norway and commemorates the signing of the Norwegian Constitution in 1814. It is celebrated with parades, flags and traditional costumes.
- Northern Norway is known for its stunning natural beauty, including the Northern Lights (Aurora Borealis) and majestic fjords.

Words From the Author

We hope that you enjoyed learning about the wonderful country of Norway.

Norway is a country rich in culture and beauty, with lots of wonderful places to visit and people to meet.

We hope you continue to learn more about this wonderful nation. If you enjoyed this book, consider leaving a review!

With Love